FINDING A FINANCIAL ADVISOR YOU CAN TRUST

A GUIDE FOR INVESTORS
(and those who want to be)

Barbara Stanny

Published in the United States of America by
Powerful Woman Press
2023 E. Sims Way, Suite 328
Port Townsend, WA 98368
www.BarbaraStanny.com

First edition, January 2007
This revised edition published 2015
Printed in the U.S.A.
ISBN-10: 1-934126-05-5
ISBN-13: 978-1-934126-05-9

CONTENTS

ACKNOWLEDGMENTS

This booklet had a previous life.

In the early 1990s, I was working as a journalist in San Francisco. Thanks to the support and encouragement of Resourceful Women (RW), a San Francisco nonprofit dedicated to the financial education of women, I had finally weathered my own financial crisis, educated myself about money, found a fabulous financial advisor and was about to write a book on women and money. That's when RW asked my friend and fellow writer, Deanne Stone, and I to create a pamphlet about finding and working with financial advisors. The result: a booklet titled *Choosing and Managing Financial Professionals: A Guide for Women Investors*. This little book found its way into the hands of hundreds of individuals through the tireless distribution efforts of RW.

Unfortunately, RW folded a few years later, and the booklet disappeared. Still, word of mouth was so strong that for over a decade, I continued to hear from people asking where they could find the booklet. In 2005, Deanne graciously gave me her generous permission to rewrite and republish this booklet. Thank you so much, Deanne.

I also want to thank some of the people, many of whom I've long lost touch with, for making the original version possible: Carol Malnick, Mort Levy, Judy Barber, Jane Lewenthal, Peter Camejo, James Demmert, Michal Feder, John Hallgren, Joyce Linker, Dave Shore, Ellen Stromberg, Tracy Gary, and Laurel Cook.

Fast forwarding to 2006, I give special thanks to Oriana Green, who came up with the idea, then encouraged me, nagged me and finally cracked her whip until I rewrote the original. I am also indebted to the financial professionals—Eileen Michaels (my wonderful financial advisor), Leanne Kraemer, Jan Goldman, and Leisa Aiken—who took the time to read the revisions, making sure everything was accurate and up to date.

INTRODUCTION

The one question I am asked more often than any other, whenever I speak to an audience, teach a workshop, or coach a client, without doubt is this: How do I find a financial advisor I can trust?

It's an excellent question. Managing money can be overwhelming to anyone who is not an expert. And believe me, even the experts need help. Sure you can choose to manage your money on your own. But if you're like the majority of people I've met (including people who work in the financial industry), you're so busy with your own complicated life that you don't have the time, let alone knowledge, skills, or interest to pay close attention to your own portfolio.

I'm a big believer in working with professionals. The challenge, of course, is finding someone you can trust.

Whether you are just starting out or you've been investing on your own for a while; whether the amount you're investing is large or small, from an inheritance or from earnings; whether you are fairly well versed in finances or your eyes glaze over at the mere mention of money, you are probably wondering some of the same things: Where do I find someone I can count on? What if I don't understand everything they tell me? Do I really need to pay someone? And, what if they lose money I can't easily make up from my earnings?

If you have these concerns, that's normal, and actually quite good if they motivate you to do something. A big secret to finding the best professional for you is to become a well-informed consumer. That means educating yourself so you can evaluate what they tell you. Over time, you will gain the knowledge you need to choose how you want to manage your money and, with it, the confidence and satisfaction that comes from making informed decisions.

The information presented here is meant to get you started. Much of what lies in the pages that follow comes from conversations with a variety of financial advisors as well as people like yourself who have moved through their fears and concerns to find a professional they trust. You will hear their voices throughout this booklet.

There are no shortcuts to becoming an informed investor; the only way to learn is by doing. How?

1. **Start educating yourself, today, right now**, before you hire a financial professional. Go to the library, talk with knowledgeable friends, listen to financial programs on radio and TV, read the business section of the newspaper, surf financial sites, flip through money magazines, attend financial workshops and seminars, start a financial study group with other women who have similar values and concerns. *If you're a novice, this might feel overwhelming*. And it may well be, at first. But stick with it.
2. **Make financial education a daily practice**, and do it in small doses. In other words, do a little something every day related to money. It doesn't need to be a big deal. Simply peruse the headlines of the business section every morning. Turn on NPR's Nightly Business Report while cooking dinner. (A word of warning: much of what you'll hear and read is sensationalism, not solid information, so take the hype with a grain of salt.) Have lunch with a friend who knows about money and pick her brain. Read one page, or even a paragraph, of say, *Financial Planning for Dummies*, before bed. Drop all your spare change into a jar at night.
3. **Commit to doing this for three months.** Follow this One-Small-Step-a-Day Plan as a starting point, and you'll be amazed how much smarter you'll become in a few months. Even if you're already knowledgeable about money, there's always more to learn.

Start today, right now. (The fact that you're reading this book counts!) As an impetus, consider what John Templeton, founder of Templeton Funds, has to say about the hazards of ignoring your money: "If inflation averages 4 percent, it will reduce the buying power of a $100,000 portfolio to $66,000 in 10 years. To maintain the same buying power, that portfolio would have to grow to $148,000 just to remain even over a decade, and this doesn't count taxes." In other words, doing nothing with your money, or not understanding your choices are both equally risky.

4. **Learn the language of investing**. I suggest you browse through the glossary at the end of the booklet before you read further. I have included definitions of the most common types of investments as well as some of the financial jargon that often confuses beginners.

"I had worked in our family business and knew the effort my father put into building it. When I got my inheritance, I felt a tremendous responsibility to do right by it. I was encouraged by several people to do nothing with my money for six months while I attended financial seminars, took classes at the local community college and read as much as I could. That initial encouragement to take it easy was the best advice I could have gotten. I felt so confident when I picked the manager I wanted to work with."

~Janice, a 39-year-old investor

PART I
LEARNING THE BASICS

> *"If you're going to invest, you have to know who the players are and what they can do for you."*
> ~Carol Malnick, investment manager

Typically, people make the same serious mistakes over and over again, especially if they're uninformed. They either ignore their finances completely, blindly turn over control to the first advisor they talk to, or become so paralyzed by fears of losing it that they keep their assets in low-yielding investments that don't keep up with inflation.

I want you to avoid these mistakes—and you can if you follow the guidelines I offer in this booklet. Working with a professional is the best way I know to get on track and *stay* on track. But please remember, no matter how good your advisors are, the ultimate responsibility for your finances always rests with you.

Q. *When do I need to see a financial professional?*

A. If you find yourself in any one of the following situations (and you will, at some point), I highly recommend that you consult a financial expert:

- You have inherited money.
- You have a complex financial and tax situation.
- You are making a major life change that will affect your financial status (marriage, divorce, widowhood).
- You need help with budgeting, reducing your taxes

or estate planning

- You need to plan for retirement.
- You need a plan for funding your children's college education.
- You are caring for elderly or incapacitated parents.
- You are concerned about outliving your savings or your inheritance.
- You want to educate yourself about investment strategies.
- You need help selecting investments or sticking to a plan.
- You want to reassess your investment strategies.
- You need to do something, but don't know where to
- start.

Q. *What are the differences among financial professionals that I should be aware of?*

A. ***Financial advisor*** is a catchall title that encompasses a range of experts—money managers, stockbrokers, financial planners, investment management consultants, accountants, estate planners, lawyers, bankers, and insurance agents. According to an aptly titled article "Alphabet Soup," in a recent edition of *The Wall Street Journal*, there are 35 different titles in financial planning, advising, and taxes. Each has some area of expertise to offer you.

In the past, these categories of advisors were sharply defined, but today many of these professionals overlap in the services they provide. Besides giving you the information, encouragement, and advice you need to invest and manage your money, these experts can serve as your teachers and coaches. At best, they can help you avoid costly mistakes. Which ones to choose and how to use them depends on your particular needs and the time and effort you are willing to spend in managing your finances.

For the purposes of this booklet, I will focus on those who offer advice on stocks, bonds, mutual funds and to a limited extent, real estate. This group consists of financial planners, stockbrokers, investment advisors and money managers.

FINANCIAL PLANNERS

Certification

The term ***financial planner*** is broadly used. Strictly speaking, only those who have taken the required two years of course work and passed a rigorous ten hour, two day exam can be licensed as Certified Financial Planners™ and use the initials CFP® after their names. You may also come across the title ChFC (Chartered Financial Consultant) or CLU (Chartered Life Underwriter), which indicates the person has been trained by the insurance industry. Chances are, they'll be focused on selling you insurance products.

But titles alone are not necessarily the best indicator of a financial planner's skill. Referrals from trustworthy professionals or knowledgeable friends may be a better starting point than the initials after their name. If you talk with friends, however, keep in mind that their needs and circumstances may be different from yours. That is why you must interview several professionals to find the right advisor for you.

What They Do

The big advantage of working with a financial planner is that they help you look at the big picture, all aspects of your financial situation, including investments, taxes, budgeting, debt, home buying, your kids' education, and insurance needs. Whether you're just beginning to think about what to do with your money or you're a sophisticated investor who needs to reevaluate her strategies, a financial planner is an excellent resource.

If you have not thought about your finances in terms of objectives, or are unsure of your goals, let that be the focus of your first meeting. It's their job to ask you the right questions. A financial planner will work with you to define your goals, and then help you identify the types of investments that suit both your goals and your tolerance for risk—a subject you will hear more about later. A good financial planner will become your partner in designing the blueprint for your future security. They'll explain various investment options available. They'll also advise you how best to allocate your assets, such as how much to put into stocks, bonds, and other investments and how much to keep in cash. Some financial planners will also recommend specific investments and, on request, refer you to various professional advisors.

You should be aware, however, that many financial planners are also certified public accountants (CPAs), or stockbrokers, or insurance agents. In those cases, they may want to provide those services for you themselves rather than refer you to other professionals.

Besides reviewing your overall financial situation, your financial planner may make sure that, among other things, your records are in order, you have sufficient insurance, and potential tax problems are detected and avoided. And periodically—quarterly or at least annually— they will meet with you to see whether you need to review your goals or change your investment strategy.

What They Charge

Financial planners have different ways of charging for their services. There are six ways to pay your advisor.

One is an hourly consultation fee. (The National

Association of Personal Financial Advisors, www.napfa.org, offers the names of fee-only professionals.)

Second is commission based, meaning that you pay them a fee each time you buy a product: stocks, mutual funds, insurance policies, limited partnerships, or annuities.

The third includes both ways; charging a fee for advising you and commissions on any securities they sell to you.

The fourth is a wrap, or assets-under-management, fee which is all-inclusive based on assets under management, including advice and transactions.

The fifth is an annual retainer fee which is often based on the complexity of your situation and the services your relationship includes.

Finally, some financial planners charge a combination of fees such as a flat fee for financial planning and an assets-under-management fee for investment management.

As with all the other types of advisors, when you buy or sell any product through a financial planner, you will receive confirmations of the transactions. Every advisor should provide you with at least quarterly reports on your holdings.

"For years I jumped in and out of the market, impulsively buying stocks I had read about in financial publications and then panicking and selling them. When I confessed to a friend how undisciplined I was, she referred me to her financial planner. He did two things that really woke me up: He drew a pie chart showing how lopsided my investments were, and he did a twenty-year income projection based on a five-percent inflation rate. I had thought I was set for life; when he showed me that if I continued as I had been I'd be broke by age 50, I was stunned. That's when I got serious about learning what I needed to know"

~Theresa, a 29-year-old executive

STOCKBROKERS/FINANCIAL ADVISORS

Certification

Stockbrokers (these days they're more often referred to as financial advisors or financial consultants) are trained by the brokerage firms that hire them. After they've been on the job three months, they must pass a rigorous exam from the National Association of Securities Dealers (NASD). Then they receive their broker's license, register with the NASD and with the state in which they do business.

What They Do

The old job of stockbrokers was simply to buy and sell securities. Traditionally, they gave investment advice and executed trades (bought and sold securities such as stocks and bonds) for individual investors. These days, however, the financial industry is going through major changes. You'll see them not just in brokerage houses, but banks, accounting firms, insurance agencies, and trust companies. To stay competitive, and meet the needs of the public, most firms sell a wider variety of products (mutual funds, annuities, exchange traded funds, etc.) and offer more services. Now it is common for brokers to act as financial planners and to execute trades for outside portfolio managers (which you will hear more about later).

If you want a financial advisor to advise you on different types of investments (stocks, bonds, mutual funds, etc.), open an account with a full-service brokerage firm. If you prefer to do your own research and select your own stocks, open an account with a discount brokerage firm which charges significantly lower commission fees than full-service brokerage houses. Discount brokers do not usually give specific recommendations, although recently a few have begun to do so in an effort to gain an edge on their competitors.

Brokerage firms have staffs of security analysts who study industry trends and research a wide range of stocks and bonds. Each month, brokerage firms publish their staff's recommendations on whether to buy, sell, or hold particular securities, and they mail those reports to their clients with their monthly account statements. You will discover, however, that selecting winners from a universe of about 10,000 stocks is uncertain at best—even for the experts. Not only do they frequently disagree with one another, but at times their educated guesses are far off the mark. Read the literature the brokerage firms send you and check out your broker's recommendations, but never rely on them as your sole source of information.

What They Charge

Commissions can vary significantly from one broker to another, so be sure to do comparison shopping. Call different brokerage firms and ask about their commissions on stock transactions. In addition, both full-service and discount brokers are usually willing to negotiate commissions, depending on the size of your portfolio and how actively you trade. And keep in mind the important distinction between brokers: full-service stockbrokers receive a large part of their income from commissions on sales of securities and other products, and discount brokers are salaried. (For a discussion of professional compensation, see Part IV.)

Each time you buy or sell a stock, you will receive a trade confirmation, and each month or quarterly your brokerage firm will send you a statement summarizing the activity in your account. Initially, you may need help in reading your monthly statements. Don't be shy about asking your broker to explain any item that is unclear to you.

MONEY MANAGERS

Certification

Money managers are also known as *Investment Managers* or *Portfolio Managers.* Any individuals who pays the fee, takes the test, and fills out the prescribed registration forms can be listed as Registered Investment Advisors (RIA) regardless of education or experience. Yet that title gives them authority to have discretion over clients' accounts. Because just about anyone can call him- or herself a money manager, the range of expertise runs the gamut from topnotch to poor.

To find the best qualified person for your needs, interview several—again, starting with referrals from trusted sources. Always inquire about their educational backgrounds, and take special note if the manager is a Chartered Financial Analyst, a title awarded after three years of rigorous course work. And be sure to ask prospective managers if they conform to reporting standards established by the Association for Investment Management and Research (AIMR). These are standards with which all money managers should comply. Ask them how much money they have under management, how long they've been in business, what their investment style is, and whether they have a published track record.

What They Do

If you do not feel competent or would prefer not to be involved with day-to-day decisions, you can hire a money manager to buy and sell securities. You hire a money manager because you trust that he or she can achieve superior performance results over a market cycle— typically three to five years.

One advantage to working with money managers is their

access to a wide range of printed and computerized reports about overall economic trends and specific companies. Furthermore, most money managers also make it a point to visit many of the companies they recommend or at least stay in touch with the company managers.

Whether money managers work independently or through brokerage houses or banks, they require a substantial minimum investment. More and more, you'll find those who have a $100,000 minimum but quite a few require an initial investment of anywhere from $250,000 to $1 million or more.

How money managers invest your money is based on clearly defined objectives you will have discussed beforehand. Unlike financial planners or stockbrokers who are obligated to get your approval before making any transactions in your name, money managers will ask you to transfer power of attorney to them, meaning that they have limited legal power to buy or sell securities without consulting you. Money managers are only concerned with the performance of your portfolio. Period. They will keep you informed of any significant changes they make in your portfolio, but they will not call you to discuss each trade.

Typically, a money manager sets up an account in your name at either a brokerage firm, bank, or trust company, which acts as the custodian of your cash and securities and the vehicle through which securities will be traded for you. When the money manager buys or sells a stock in your account, he or she calls the brokerage firm to carry out the trade.

If you have more than $500,000 to invest, you may consider using more than one money manager. Money managers have different philosophies, styles, and areas of specialization. For example, if one of your managers takes an aggressive approach to investing, you may want to balance that person's style with the more conservative approach of a second manager. In the same vein, you may choose managers specializing in different industries or in different types of corporations, such as blue chips or small, start-up companies. When you divide your money between managers you gain more diversification, but you may lose some leverage in negotiating fees. However, if your account is held at one firm that works with outside money managers, fees may be discounted.

Before signing on with any money manager, be sure to ask about his or her policy regarding termination of contract. Every once in a while you may come across a manager who has an unreasonable advance notification policy of two or three months. Don't even consider agreeing to that.

What They Charge

The annual fees money managers charge depend on the size of your account. Generally, the more money you give them to manage, the smaller your fee. For example, a money manager may charge a 2.5 percent fee to manage an account under $250,000, a 1 percent fee for $1 million, and a .5 percent fee for an account of $5 million or more. As a rule of thumb, a 2 percent fee is considered high and a 1 percent fee reasonable. A major criterion in selecting a money manager is whether that person can manage the portfolio in good and bad markets to minimize or diminish risk, and protect your investment. Besides the annual fee, in some cases you may also pay commission on the stocks you buy and sell. As an alternative to paying brokerage firm commissions on each trade executed by your money manager, you may elect to pay the brokerage firm a fee that is a percentage of the value of your account. That fee covers all expenses of transactions and reporting, as well as advising. (This arrangement is different from a wrap account, which I will discuss later.) These commissions are significantly lower than what you would pay as an individual investor because money managers trade in large volume and receive discounts from the brokerage firms. Your manager will send you a monthly or quarterly statement and a quarterly performance report that evaluates his or her results.

INVESTMENT MANAGEMENT CONSULTANTS

A growing number of financial advisors now specialize in matching clients with money managers. These consultants can spare you the effort of doing all the legwork entailed in evaluating and choosing the right money managers. Once you have chosen a money manager, the consultant will continue to monitor and evaluate his or her performance to make sure your best interests are being served. The consultant, in essence, acts as your advocate to ensure that your manager is giving you the service you deserve. But again let me remind you: hiring an investment management consultant does not relieve you of personal responsibility. You still must oversee your own finances.

OTHER OPTIONS

If you want professional management but can't or don't want to meet the minimum investment most independent money managers demand, you have other options: wrap accounts and mutual funds, both of which can be overseen by a financial advisor.

WRAP ACCOUNTS

Brokerage firms created wrap accounts to compete with the burgeoning mutual fund industry. Many investors like them because they provide professional management and require a smaller minimum to open an account.

The reason they are called wrap accounts is because brokerage firms take all the commissions and other administrative fees you would otherwise be charged for buying and selling stocks and bonds individually and wrap them together into one fee. That means no matter how many or how few trades the manager makes in your account, your fee stays the same.

Brokerage firms charge an annual 1— 2 percent flat fee of assets managed, although they are usually willing to negotiate a lower fee on larger accounts. The brokerage firms use teams of in-house managers or contract with outside money managers to handle wrap accounts for their clients. The flat fee you pay is divided among your broker, the firm, and the money managers. If the idea of a wrap account interests you, start by calling one or more brokerage firms to set up appointments.

If you already work with a financial advisor, ask him or her to recommend money managers for you to consider based on your investment goals and tolerance for risk. Once you have evaluated their performance records, you will be able to choose the one whose investment strategy and style matches yours. (For suggestions on interviewing, see PART II.)

Remember, a wrap account is only as good as the manager, so it is important for you to take an active role in selecting the money management firm responsible for your investments. Some questions you should ask the broker are:

- What can a wrap account offer me that a mutual fund can't?
- How does the brokerage firm select its money managers?
- Can you go over their performance records with me?

- What is your basis for recommending these managers to me?
- Do I communicate with the managers only through you, or are there times when I can talk to them directly?
- What happens when there is a change of management?

Your advisor, not the money manager, will send you periodic reports on the performance of your portfolio. As with any other advisor, it is your responsibility to monitor the performance of your wrap account manager.

MUTUAL FUNDS

Another way to obtain professional management of your investments is to buy a mutual fund. As in a wrap account, an expert manages your money, but in a mutual fund your money is pooled with that of thousands of other investors. The professional manager invests the pooled money in stocks, bonds, or other instruments, depending on the objective of the fund. You become a shareholder of the fund, with the number of shares you own depending on how much money you invested.

Mutual funds are phenomenally popular today, and for good reasons. For one, they require relatively small initial investments—usually between $1,000 and $2,500. If you agree to make monthly automated payments, you may be able to start with as little as $50. And you can increase your stake in the fund at any time, either by requesting that your dividends be reinvested rather than paid directly to you or by buying additional shares on a monthly or quarterly basis. Second, assuming you have checked his or her track record, you benefit from the expertise of the fund's manager. Third, mutual funds may offer more diversification than most people can afford investing as individuals.

The advantage of diversification is that you get to participate in a wide range of stocks while limiting your downside risk—that is, the risk that all the stocks in the portfolio will perform poorly at the same time. Despite diversification, the share value of mutual funds still fluctuates with the ups and downs of the market and the investing strategy of the mutual fund manager. For example, an aggressive fund that rises 30 percent in an up market may fall 30 percent or more in a down market; a conservative fund, on the other hand, may fluctuate only 5 or 10 percent. You can check the value of funds in the daily mutual fund listings in the financial section of the *Wall Street Journal* (www.wsj.com), your local paper or on the Internet.

Mutual funds are geared to the varied needs of investors. You can choose funds that have different levels of risk (high, moderate, or low) and different objectives (growth, income, tax-free income, and aggressive growth). You can also buy funds called *sector funds* that invest within specific industries, such as telecommunications, utilities, gold or real estate, although these funds tend to be more volatile because of their narrower focus.

Mutual funds fall into two main categories: load and no-load funds. Load funds carry a sales charge of anywhere from 1 percent to 3 percent. By contrast, no-load funds have no sales charge and their management fees tend to be low. With so many high-performing no-load funds, many investors ask, why pay a premium to buy a load fund?

Let's compare what happens when you invest $10,000 in a load or no-load mutual fund. If you buy a no-load fund, your $10,000 goes to work for you immediately, but if you buy a load fund with a 3 percent sales charge, you pay a $300 commission. That means your initial investment is actually $9,700. Each time you make additional contributions to your load fund, the commission is subtracted from the amount you invest.

Despite the advantages of no-load funds, some investors think it is a mistake to completely ignore load funds. For example, some load funds have earned exceptionally high returns that more than offset the fees, and some no-load funds have turned in mediocre results. Also, there may be hidden expenses in those no-load funds. As a rule of thumb, when choosing among mutual funds first consider your objective; second, check the track record of the current portfolio manager; and last, compare the commissions and fees of similar funds.

You can buy (and sell) shares of mutual funds through a financial planner, bank, or stockbroker who will charge you a commission on each transaction, though many have waived transaction fees for certain no-load mutual fund groups. Alternatively, no-load shares can be purchased directly from the fund company – that is, the company that originated the fund – without your having to pay a commission.

Many people who own shares in several mutual funds still prefer to buy additional no-load shares through their broker, even though they have to pay small commissions on each transaction. For one, it's more convenient; you can trade funds by making one telephone call to the brokerage firm rather than by calling the individual companies. Second, the brokerage firms report all transactions and dividend distributions from the different funds in consolidated monthly statements. (When you buy shares directly from the fund companies, you have to keep track of the statements on your own.)

Choosing a mutual fund is not easy. With more than 8,000 funds available, even sophisticated investors need help in evaluating them. I suggest you seek recommendations from your financial planner or read publications that evaluate mutual funds.

COMPARISON OF INVESTMENT MANAGEMENT OPTIONS

	Self	**Broker**	**Money Manager**	**Mutual Fund**
Minimum investment	none	none	$100,000 to $5 million	$50 to $2,500
Client involvement	high	medium	low	low
Fees charged	comm.	comm. or fee	fee	comm. (load fund) minor fees (no-load)
Record keeping requirement	high	low	low	low
(comm. = commission)				

PART II
DOING YOUR HOMEWORK

> *"Many people go to a financial advisor and say, 'Here's my money'. Then six months down the road these same people are disappointed by their returns because they didn't know what their goals were. I'd like to see people asking themselves some questions before they start investing."*
> ~James Demmert, money manager

As I noted, your selection of a financial professional depends on how much money you want to invest, how active you intend to be in the investment decisions, and your personal needs, goals, and tolerance for risk. The first advisor you hire may be perfect when you are starting out but not the right person when you become a more sophisticated investor. Over time, as your circumstances change, so may your choice of advisors.

Q. *How should I prepare before interviewing advisors?*

A. If you aren't clear about what you want and need, it will be difficult for any professional to advise you. And it will be even more difficult for you to evaluate what they tell you. So you need to do some homework before you talk to any professional.

HOMEWORK QUESTIONS

1. **How much money do I have to invest?**
2. **What are my financial goals?**
3. **What kind of risks am I willing to take?**
4. **What should I know about myself that may affect my choice of advisors?**

5. How can I assure that my investment decisions reflect my personal values?
6. How much should I know about investments before talking to a professional?

Let's tackle these one by one.

1. How much money do I have to invest?

Before you can answer this question, you need to know your net worth (see worksheets). First, add up your assets (everything you own, except this won't include your home in terms of investable assets). Then, subtract your liabilities (everything you owe). What is left is your net worth -what you would have in hand if you converted all your assets into cash and paid off all your debts. Remember, this formula gives you an estimate only. You don't know what an asset is worth until you sell it. After you know your net worth, decide how much "untouchable" money you want to set aside for emergencies in a money market fund or short term CDs. Now you should have a better idea of how much money you want to invest.

2. What are my financial goals?

No one expects you to know your goals for the rest of your life, but you can make some guesses as to what you want in the next five years. Do you need your investments to generate income for living expenses? Or do you want to invest for growth, for instance to save for your children's college education or to buy a house? Unless you set some goals, neither you nor your advisor can know which investments to include in your portfolio. Clear timelines— knowing how much money you need and by when— are a critical ingredient for making prudent choices. Don't worry about being locked into these goals; you can always change your priorities—and you will.

Calculating your net worth

ASSETS

Cash (or equivalents)

Cash in checking and savings accounts	$__________
Money market funds	$__________
Cash value of life insurance	$__________
Loans recievable	$__________
Other	$__________

Investments (market value)

Certificates of deposit	$__________
Stocks	$__________
Bonds	$__________
Mutual funds	$__________
Annuities	$__________

Retirement funds

IRAs	$__________
401(k), 403(b), 457 Plans	$__________
Pension/profit-sharing plan	$__________
Other	$__________

Real estate (current market value)

Residence	$__________
Income property	$__________
Land	$__________

Self-employed Business valuation (net) $__________

Personal property

Automobiles	$__________
Recreational Vehicle/Boat	$__________
Household furnishings	$__________
Collections/Art	$__________
Jewelry	$__________
Other	$__________

TOTAL ASSETS $__________

LIABILITIES

Current Debts

Credit Cards $______________

Department store cards $______________

Medical $______________

Back taxes $______________

Other $______________

Loans

Personal (Bank/finance companies) $______________

Home equity $______________

Education $______________

Automobile $______________

Recreational Vehicle/Boat $______________

Personal (from friends/family) $______________

Other $______________

Mortgages

Home(s) $______________

Investment properties $______________

Land $______________

Other $______________

Total Liabilities $______________

Net worth calculation

TOTAL ASSETS (from page 22) $______________

Minus TOTAL LIABILITIES $______________

Equals Net Worth $______________

> *"My dream is to live abroad for a few years. I've worked out a plan of dollar-cost averaging—putting the same amount of money each month into several growth mutual funds. If all goes well, in six years I'll be able to quit my job."*
> ~Andrea, 44 year old teacher

3. What kind of risks am I willing to take?

Knowing your tolerance for risk is perhaps the most crucial information you as an investor can provide to your financial advisor. In this context, risk refers to market volatility. In other words, the amount of uncertainty that accompanies inevitable market plunges you are willing to assume to achieve a particular financial objective.

To assess your risk tolerance, ask yourself: Can I sleep at night if my stocks move up and down like a roller coaster? Am I willing to tolerate that volatility in the hope of earning high returns? Or would I feel more secure owning stocks that grow slowly but fluctuate less? Remember, bonds also oscillate, though those swings don't matter if you hold the bond to maturity. But be aware, bonds may be "called" and not held to maturity.

Keep in mind: ***the biggest risk you take is that you will outlive your money, and that your money will not grow as fast as inflation and taxes eat it away.*** Putting all your money in a savings account or under the mattress is a sure fire recipe for losing future spending power. At least some of your money needs to be in assets that will grow faster than inflation and taxes. Your comfort level, along with education, is your best guide in choosing types of investments and their allocation. For example:

- If you have a high tolerance for risk, and a long time for growth, you may want to invest most of your money in stocks.

- If you want growth without too much risk, you'll want to add some bonds to your portfolio.
- If your goal is to conserve your principal with minimum risk, you may hold a few stocks but put the majority of your money in bonds and cash-equivalent investments, such as money market funds, short-term certificates and Treasury bills. But remember, if you're too conservative, you'll lose purchasing power to inflation.

4. What should I know about myself before selecting advisors?

A little self-scrutiny before you begin your search will pay off later. If you tend to be disorganized or lack follow-through, you will want to find a financial professional willing to teach you how to maintain good records and keep you on track. Or, if you prefer to do your own research but still want to talk to someone about your stock picks, you'll want to find a trustworthy broker with whom you can cultivate that kind of relationship. The key to investing, as in everything you do, is to *know yourself*. The inventory sheet will help you to create a picture of your strengths and weaknesses.

SELF-INVENTORY

Assuming O is the mid-point, put an X where you fall on the continuum between each pair of attributes.

-O-

cautious ________________________________ impulsive
thrifty ________________________________ extravagant
organized ________________________________disorganized
suspicious ________________________________ trusting
patient ________________________________ impatient
indirect ________________________________ direct
indecisive ________________________________ decisive
focused ________________________________ unfocused
pessimistic ________________________________ optimistic
inner-directed ________________________ outer-directed
diligent ________________________________ lax
defeatist ________________________________ resilient

You may detect patterns to your answers that you were unaware of, or your answers may confirm what you already know about yourself. What, if anything, is relevant to you as an investor?

5. How can I assure that my investment decisions reflect my personal values?

When you apply socially responsible criteria to your investments, you are, in effect, voting with your dollars. There are two ways you can screen investments. You can choose to exclude companies that make large profits from products you do not wish to support such as alcohol, tobacco, weapons, or nuclear power. Or you can take a more proactive approach and seek out those companies that contribute to society by protecting the environment, providing child care, treating women and minorities equitably, enforcing strong affirmative-action policies, and/or supporting social programs in the communities in which they do business.

If socially responsible investing is important to you, be sure you hire an advisor who shares your values, or at least is willing to honor them. Not all money managers are willing to do the extra research involved in screening stocks.

If you prefer not to use socially responsible screens, you can use your money to express your values in other ways. One obvious choice is to simply write checks to nonprofit organizations whose work you value. Another possibility is to develop a strategy for providing long-term support to those organizations. For example, you can make a nonprofit organization the beneficiary of your estate or insurance policy. Or, you can educate yourself about what professionals call "planned giving." Ask your lawyer or financial planner to explain the pros and cons of charitable lead trusts or charitable remainder trusts. They can also explain other options, such as setting up donor-advised funds within community foundations or forming private foundations. Making contributions through trusts and foundations can save you and your estate money.

6. How much should I know about investments before talking to a professional?

Keep in mind that your ultimate goal is to clearly understand your financial situation. That does not mean that you will have to research and select all your own investments, nor does it mean you have to have all the answers. What it does mean is that you have to be sufficiently well informed to evaluate the advice your financial professional gives you. And if you don't understand what they tell you, keep asking until you do. Education now could save you a lot of sorrow down the road.

PART III
BEGINNING THE SEARCH

> *"Your purpose in interviewing professionals is not to look for someone who gives you all the right answers, but rather to listen for warning signs. The interview is your opportunity to get to know the person and to decide if the two of you are a relatively good match."*
> ~Jane Lewenthal, financial advisor

Two mistakes investors make in hiring financial professionals are *failing to interview more than one advisor* and *neglecting to verify their references*. Another mistake, and the most overlooked, is *not taking responsibility*; like not reading statements, not asking questions, not going to meetings and not updating your plan. When clients tell advisor Eileen Michaels they aren't worried and they trust her, she always responds, "Don't!" The reason is, she says, "It's their money, and this is a partnership." Most cases of financial mismanagement could be avoided if investors carefully checked out their advisors and kept tabs on them for the duration. Finding the right person starts with the interview.

INTERVIEWING TIPS

Approach the interviews with the attitude that this is your money and that you're hiring someone to work for you. Honestly, *there are no dumb questions*. Your job is to learn as much as you can, so don't be shy about asking questions—and repeating questions if you don't understand their responses—until you have all the information you need to make good decisions.

If you have never interviewed a financial advisor before and feel intimidated before you start, consider asking a friend who has gone through the process to act as your coach. When you feel confident enough to handle your own interviews, call for your first appointment.

Take a notebook to every interview and record the professional's answers and your impressions. Later, review your notes and, if you have more questions, call back. After finishing your interviews, review your notes again. This is the time to take a hard look at whether the advisor responded to the questions you asked. *Your best guide is your gut*. No matter how smart, capable or highly-recommended someone may be, if you don't feel "right" do NOT hire that person. Always, always, always trust your intuition.

Some women feel beholden to advisors who take extra time to answer their questions. Please don't let that influence you. Initial free consultations are part of a professional advisor's business. Regardless of how much they would like it, they don't expect everyone they talk with to become their clients.

Q. *How many advisors should I plan to interview?*

A. Getting referrals from friends and advisors is only the first step. The second, and most important, step is asking them the right questions. I suggest that you begin by interviewing three financial advisors; any more could become confusing. If you do not know anyone who can refer you to financial professionals, you may have to start by calling a professional association that licenses financial advisors. But remember, in most cases these sources can assure you only that an individual has met certain licensing or professional requirements; they don't help you to differentiate one advisor from another.

When calling for a consultation, find out whether the person charges for this exploratory visit. Most don't. You can avoid any misunderstandings by telling them at your first meeting that you are interviewing several people. If you don't feel compatible with any of those you interviewed, try contacting another three. Keep interviewing until you find someone you like, trust and feel is knowledgeable.

Q. *What questions should I ask?*

A. The list below suggests some basic territory you should cover in your interviews. You can add your own questions to this list. Feel free to ask as many questions as necessary to help you understand what you need to know.

INTERVIEWING QUESTIONS

1. **Would you tell me about yourself?**
2. **Do you specialize in certain investments?**
3. **Who are your clients?**
4. **How do you charge for your services, and what costs might I incur working with you?**
5. **How often do you communicate with clients, and how often might I expect to hear from you?**
6. **How do you handle your own investment mistakes?**
7. **Have you ever been involved in any lawsuits, arbitration, or disciplinary problems?**
8. **Is there anything you want me to know about you that I haven't asked?**

Let's discuss each question in turn.

1. Would you tell me about yourself?

It's always a good idea to begin an interview with a question that opens the door for the other person to start talking freely. What you're listening for in their answers is information about their education, their years of experience and their investment philosophy. Their responses will suggest other questions you can ask, such as whether they tend to trade stocks frequently or hold on to them for the longer term, and whether they vary their investment strategy under different market conditions, such as when the market is flat, falling or rising.

2. Do you specialize in certain investments?

Advisors may specialize in mutual funds, individual stocks and bonds or products such as real estate mortgages, insurance policies, and tax-deferred annuities. You are looking for an advisor who specializes in the areas in which you want to invest. Listen for specific information. You don't want an advisor who talks in generalities.

3. Who are your clients?

Listen to find out whether the investors they describe share your general goals and concerns and whether you fit in with the advisor's clientele.

4. How do you charge for your services, and what costs might I incur working with you?

Always ask financial planners whether they are compensated by a flat fee, commission, or percentage of assets. Ask financial advisors under what conditions they might be willing to negotiate their commissions. Ask money managers what their fees are and whether they are negotiable.

5. How often do you communicate with your clients, and how often may I expect to hear from you?

Some professionals prefer sticking to the business of researching and trading securities. Rather than taking time to meet in person with their clients, they keep in touch through quarterly newsletters or reports. If you want more hand-holding, mention when you are interviewing that you need someone you can feel free to call, whether to ask questions or calm your nerves. Not all professionals have the inclination or personality to accommodate your requests.

6. How do you handle your own investment mistakes?

Again, the answer to this question depends on the professional you're interviewing. No advisor—no matter how sterling his or her record—avoids choosing losers occasionally. Anyone who tells you otherwise either hasn't been in business long or is lying. What you want to find out is the person's philosophy about handling losing investments: Under what circumstances do they hold on to a falling stock, or cut their losses and sell?

7. Have you ever been involved in any lawsuits, arbitration or disciplinary problems?

Advisors, by law, are required to give you an honest answer. You can ask to see a copy of their Form ADV, which will inform you of any violations or disciplinary actions. You can also check out a certified financial planner's disciplinary record at www.cfpboard.net. Smaller advisors, with less than $25 million under management, are regulated by their specific state. That information is available at www.nasaa.org. Another resource is: www.finra.org.

8. Is there anything you want me to know about you that I haven't asked?

This is another open-ended question that often elicits the most revealing answers, so pay close attention.

PART IV
MAKING CHOICES

> *"As a rule of thumb, if someone just doesn't seem right, I reject them. What's more, if something sounds too good to be true, it probably is."*
> ~Joyce Linker, financial advisor

Once you have completed your interviews, your next step is to decide which professionals to hire. In this section, you'll find five criteria you can use.

CRITERIA FOR CHOOSING FINANCIAL ADVISORS

1. **Knowledge**
2. **Track record**
3. **Investment style**
4. **Compensation**
5. **Compatibility and trust**

1. Knowledge

Your advisors should have solid educational backgrounds, broad knowledge of the world of finance, and specialized training in the investment areas that most interest you. In addition, they should have at least five years of experience and ready access to a wide range of information sources.

2. Track record

You can check the track records only of money managers and mutual funds. Financial planners and advisors tend to invest differently for each client depending on their needs, risk tolerance and goals, which means very different returns. The only way you can evaluate them is by talking to clients who have used their services.

Evaluating track records can be tricky. First, if you don't know what to look for, you can easily be misled by the numbers a money manager or mutual fund provide. Second, while track records provide useful data about how money or fund managers have performed to date, they do not guarantee future success. No money manager can consistently predict the direction in which the market will move or when it will reach its highs or lows. There are just too many unpredictable variables—fluctuations in the value of the dollar, rising interest rates and natural disasters, to name a few. Moreover, stock and bond markets move in cycles, making it difficult for any professional to earn consistently high returns year in and year out.

Nonetheless, you can get an idea of how well your money manager or mutual fund managers are doing by comparing their figures to stock indexes like the Standard & Poor's (S&P) 500 Stock Index that measures the performance of the stocks of the 500 largest, most established corporations. But at the same time, your objective is to maximize performance and limit risk. So keep in mind that diversification and asset allocation are critical components of portfolio management.

As noted, when you assess your managers' track records, it is important to judge their performance over a three-to-five year cycle because that period of time generally covers good and bad years. Look at how they did during the extended bear (falling) markets, 1972-74, 1981-82, 2001-04 and 2007-09. And also look at their record in 1987 when the markets plunged. They probably lost money like everyone else, but what you want to know is how quickly their performance results rebounded. Beware of money managers and advisors who, if they have never been through an extended bear market, believe, and may lead you to believe, that the market always bounces back quickly—say, as it did in 1987. The market always revives, but sometimes you have a long wait.

To understand some of the traps novices fall into in evaluating track records, let's look at mutual funds. If you read the advertisements for mutual funds, you will notice that many rank themselves as top performers. How can so many mutual funds be number one? The answer is in the fine print. Usually, somewhere at the bottom of the page, the ad will state which group of funds they are comparing themselves to. Funds with less impressive records often mislead the public by placing themselves in an obscure category in which they can legitimately claim to be number one. Luckily, you can turn to a reliable publication like *Morningstar Mutual Funds,* the bible for mutual fund investors, to get an impartial analysis of a fund's record.

Unfortunately, there is no equivalent public source for evaluating individual money managers. The difficulty in evaluating their results is that they use different criteria for measuring their returns. For example, some managers do not subtract clients' fees and expenses in figuring returns, a practice that inflates the actual appreciation of a client's portfolio. Be sure you understand whether the quoted returns were calculated before or after clients' fees were deducted.

Because interpreting a money manager's performance results takes a certain sophistication, I recommend you ask a knowledgeable and neutral advisor to look over the numbers with you.

3. Investment style

It's critical to choose someone who shares your investment philosophy and values and whose style is compatible with yours. If you need a specific amount of income from your assets and do not like volatility, you will want to hire an advisor or manager who specializes in blue chip stocks and low-risk bonds. If you want to gamble on larger returns and don't need income from your investments, you may want to hire an advisor who invests in smaller companies that are more volatile but have a high potential for growth.

4. Compensation

Financial professionals earn their living either by charging fees, commissions or a combination of the two. Advisors, like the rest of us, deserve to be paid for their work. Just because professionals work on commissions does not mean, necessarily, that you should suspect their recommendations. Rather, you should be aware of the potential for conflict of interest.

If you feel transactions are being made too frequently in your account, you may discuss this with your advisor and explore other ways of compensating them, such as wrap fees. For your protection, before opening an account at a full-service brokerage firm, ask a trusted friend or professional to recommend brokers they know to be reputable and knowledgeable. And always do enough of your own homework to recognize when a broker is giving you bad advice. A good starting place is asking your broker to send you reports on the company from his or her firm's research department and from *Value Line,* one of the most respected sources for evaluating the performance of individual stocks.

Financial planners who work on commission also have an extra incentive for selling particular products and proprietary funds (funds that are created and sold by their particular firm).

When you buy or sell stocks and bonds through a financial planner or broker, the commissions you pay are listed on each of your confirmation statements. **Other commissions, however, are hidden.** For example, some are paid directly to the brokerage firm or financial planner by insurance companies, limited partnerships or mutual fund families promoting their products. As the client, you have no way of knowing what, if any, compensation the advisor receives for selling those products. That does not necessarily men that the product they recommend to you is not good—only that you need to evaluate it more carefully.

There are so many good advisors that in my experience, if you do your homework and carefully interview them, you'll be fine. Occasionally, you may encounter brokers or financial planners more motivated by a desire to fill their own pockets than to serve you. But more often than not, you'll find ethical professionals who want to cultivate long-term relationships with clients.

5. Compatibility and trust

How do you feel about your prospective advisors is crucial. You want someone who gives you the information you need and in a way you can easily understand. You'll find that some advisors give you too much or too little information and others talk in jargon. You want an advisor whose style of communication matches your. And, of course, you must like the person you'll be working with. Beyond feeling comfortable with your advisors, you also must have confidence in their judgment. You'd be surprised to know how many clients pay for a professional's advice and then don't follow it.

"I interviewed several people before hiring my first advisor. At first I liked her, but after we started working together I felt frustrated because she didn't listen to me. Eventually I fired her.

Instead of feeling depressed about making a bad choice, I actually felt empowered because I acted on my gut feeling. I thought, 'Hey, I'm the client and she isn't giving me what I want, so I'll find someone else.'"
~Donna, a 36-year-old single mother

Now that you've thought about what you want from your advisors, let's see what it is they want from you.

DREAM CLIENT

- Thinks about her personal and financial goals
- Keeps a current list of her assets, their value, her cash flow and expenses
- Reviews her statements monthly
- Reports immediately any changes affecting her financial situation
- Makes clear agreements and holds to them Says clearly and directly what's on her mind
- Admits what she doesn't know and asks for help
- Comes to meetings with a list of questions and concerns
- Respects my time
- Takes action
- Expresses her appreciation

NIGHTMARE CLIENT

- Never figures out what her goals are
- Is overly trusting or overly suspicious
- Is vague and indecisive
- Won't admit what she doesn't know and never asks questions

- Never reads her monthly statements or transaction slips
- Frequently misplaces her investment records
- Never checks in and then feels neglected
- Doesn't say what's really on her mind
- Is demanding and unappreciative
- Withdraws her account without first discussing her concerns

PART V
MONITORING YOUR ADVISORS

> *"If you don't manage your money yourself, you must monitor your manager."*
> ~Judy Barber, psychotherapist and specialist in the psychology of money

Overseeing your investments takes time and discipline. Occasionally you may be tempted to let your advisors take care of everything for you. **Promise yourself you will never give in to that impulse.** Everyone you hire must be accountable to you, and you must keep tabs on each one of them. The better organized you are, the easier time you will have monitoring your advisors and staying on top of your investments.

FIVE WAYS TO OVERSEE YOUR INVESTMENTS

1 **Keep good records**
2 **Examine all statements**
3 **Measure the performance of your portfolio against industry standards and personal needs**
4 **Meet with your advisor regularly**
5 **Keep your advisors in touch with one another**

1. Keep good records

Your financial planner may have some record-keeping suggestions. Here are some I've found useful:

- Make separate files for every person you work with and for each investment you own, or use a three-ring binder with different sections for monthly statements and reports on each account.
- Save transaction slips in a small, expandable file.
- Store all documents in a fireproof file cabinet.
- Open and read your mail as soon as it arrives. Don't let it pile up, or you will be even less inclined to read it. File papers immediately. Ask your advisor which ones you can throw away. Even if your statements are paperless, be sure to read carefully.
- Keep a running list of the securities you own and give a copy to your tax preparer. Make six columns to record the name of the stock, the number of shares, the date of purchase, the price you paid, the date of sale and the price you received.
- Take notes on every conversation you have with your advisor, and keep them in a loose-leaf notebook. That way if you work with several professionals you can give a section to each one. Or, if you prefer, you can keep separate notebooks.
- Make lists of any questions or concerns you want to talk over with each professional and save them in your notebooks for your next appointment.
- Do your financial work at a time of day when you think most clearly.
- If you are not organized, consider hiring a bookkeeper, a personal assistant, or a professional organizer.

"I hired a financial planner because I don't have the discipline to stay on top of all this paperwork. I have good intentions, but I find a million ways to avoid doing what I have to do. Meeting quarterly with my advisor forces me to get organized. And then when I leave her, I always have a list of things I have to follow up on. I need someone to impose deadlines on me and to give me assignments. Maybe I spent too many years as a graduate student!"
~Louise, a 52-year-old professor

2. Examine all statements

Even if you have an assistant to help you file and locate your statements, you still need to read every statement and look over each transaction slip. It's a good idea to develop the habit of doing that the day you receive them. If you don't understand something, no matter how small, call and ask for clarification. If you still don't understand, make an appointment to meet with your advisor in person.

If you get a flurry of transaction slips from your broker, for example, don't just file them away. Examine them carefully to be sure you ordered those trades. Occasionally, brokerage firms make errors. For example, if your broker records the wrong code number or symbol for a stock transaction, you will find yourself the owner of a stock you didn't select. **It's your responsibility to detect the error and notify the broker immediately.** And it's the broker's responsibility to correct the error and pay out of his or her pocket for any losses incurred.

Typically, errors result from honest mistakes, but occasionally you may hear about unscrupulous brokers who made trades in accounts without their clients' permission. Acting without your permission is illegal; only you can authorize a buy or sell order, unless you give your advisor discretion to do so.

"The amount of mail that comes in every day is staggering. Around the time of annual reports and proxies, it's an absolute avalanche. Half the time my desk is buried under financial statements and reports. The best thing I ever did was hire a bookkeeper who created a system for organizing all my paperwork. What a difference!"

~Gloria, a 48-year-old sales manager

3. Measure the performance of your portfolio against industry standards

If you don't know how to compare the performance of your portfolio to the S&P 500, ask the professionals you hired to teach you. Sometimes, however, the comparison won't apply or there are more appropriate benchmarks. Your active participation shows them that you intend to hold them accountable.

4. Meet with your advisor regularly

This is your time to ask questions and express any fears or concerns you may have. If you have complaints, stick to specifics. For example, "My portfolio is down 5 percent. Why?" And when you're pleased with their performance, be sure to tell them that, too.

5. Keep your advisors in touch with one another

Over time, you may find yourself working with several kinds of professional advisors—an estate planning attorney, bookkeeper, a CPA, an insurance agent, a realtor—in addition to your financial advisors. You will want these advisors to confer whenever you face major changes in your financial situation (such as starting a new business or selling a property for a large capital gain). And you may want them to check in with each other periodically just to be sure they are equally well-informed about your circumstances. Plus, such teams provide you with built-in checks and balances to keep you protected.

PART VI
TRUSTING YOUR INSTINCTS

> *"If you've done your homework well, you should be in good hands. If you have any doubts about your financial professional, check them out with someone you can trust."*
> ~Mort Levy, investor advocate

Once you begin to invest, you may feel some uneasiness about the responsibilities you have assumed or about some aspect of your relationship with your advisors. Don't push those feelings aside. Instead, regard them as warning signs that require your immediate attention. Here are some common situations and suggestions for handling them.

Q. *What if I inherited financial professionals from my family and don't want to continue working with them?*

A. If you don't like their personality, values or investment style, find someone else. Remember, it's your money now and you need to do what is right for you. You may find it more difficult to dismiss advisors who are old family friends, but if you tell them honestly that you want to choose your own advisor, most likely they will wish you well.

Q. *Do I have to sign a contract with my financial advisor? I'm afraid of getting myself into something I can't easily get out of.*

A. You will have to sign a contract with any investment advisor or brokerage firm to do business with them. **The inviolable rule, of course, is never to sign any document you do not thoroughly understand.** Always take your time and if any point is unclear, ask questions. For extra protection, you should review the contract with a knowledgeable friend or attorney before signing it.

Q. *Every time my advisor calls suggesting that I buy something, I think to myself, does she really believe this is a good investment or is she just after a commission?*

A. If you feel unsure about the motives of an advisor working on commission, you need to ask yourself: Do I generally suspect people are trying to take advantage of me, or is there something about this particular advisor that makes me uneasy? Sometimes those who grow up in wealthy families learn to be distrustful of others' motives— and often with good reason. If you tend to worry that people are more interested in your money than in your welfare, use this as an opportunity to examine when those feelings are justified and when they aren't. If you think the problem is with the advisor, discuss your concerns with that person, and then review the reasons for your concerns and the advisor's responses with a trusted friend or professional. And, of course, you can switch to a fee-only financial planner or a wrap account that's inclusive of all fees.

Q. *What if my advisor pressures me to buy something?*

A. If someone tells you, "Buy this now—the price will never be this low again," or, "This stock will hit 100 in six months," your antennae should go up. Never buckle under pressure. Think seriously about changing advisors. As one money manager put it,

"There's always another stock and there's always another day."

Q. *The value of my portfolio is going down instead of up, and I think my broker is at fault. Is there any chance I can recover my losses?*

A. Yes. If your broker or other investment advisors have recommended unsuitable investments and failed to explain their risks, churned your account, or bought securities without your permission, you can file a claim against them. Your advisor is generally required to settle the dispute by arbitration. I suggest you discuss your case with a lawyer or other professionals who represent clients in disputes with brokers.

Q. *What if I want to change advisors?*

A. Before you walk away, give your current advisor a chance to respond to your complaints. Sometimes just hearing the other person's explanation can clear the air and preserve a working relationship. If after you've talked you still want to take your business elsewhere, find a new advisor who will arrange to transfer your investments for you. Then tell your advisor you want to close your account. Switching brokers should be a simple process, especially if all your holdings are commonly traded stocks, bonds, and mutual funds that are easily moved from one brokerage firm to another. Simply provide copies of your holdings at the old brokerage firm and give it to the new advisor who will take care of preparing transfer paperwork for you to sign. If you're changing money managers, the process can be slightly more complicated. Often money managers will give you a pro-rated refund and retain a fee covering 30 days.

Q. *How do I handle feeling overwhelmed or guilty about having inherited money?*

A. You're not alone. A lot of inheritors feel this way. Try talking about these conflicts with your financial planner. If you feel deeply troubled, though, you may prefer to contact trained professionals sensitive to the issues of inherited wealth. They can help you examine your attitudes and beliefs about money, self-worth, guilt, or any of the different conflicts that beset women inheritors, in particular.

PART VII
SUMMING UP

I hope that reading this booklet has convinced you that, with a little effort, you can learn the basics of investing. As in all aspects of life, your greatest satisfaction will come from knowing you can rely on your own judgment. Only then will you have achieved a genuine feeling of freedom and security.

For more resources, including an archive of articles, tips and success stories, please visit www.BarbaraStanny.com.

REMINDERS

1. **Select knowledgeable and ethical advisors**
2. **Start small**
3. **Think long term**
4. **Diversify**
5. **Don't be afraid to make mistakes**
6. **Be generous with yourself and others**

1. Select knowledgeable and ethical advisors

"I spent a lot of time searching for the right financial advisor and it's paid off. She was my mentor when I needed coaching and remains my advocate, checking in with the different money managers I've used, monitoring their performances, and generally looking out for me. I've done very, very well"
~Marcia, a 46-year-old nurse

2. Start small

"I started out making small, conservative investments. As the investments increased in value, I grew bolder. I put more money

in slightly more risky investments and doubled my original investment. I get a particular pleasure from looking at my financial picture because I know that I drew it."
~Candice, a 61-year-old retired business owner

3. Think long term

"Once I decided I was in for the long haul, the dips in the market didn't scare me so much. Instead of trading haphazardly as I used to, I follow the investment strategy I mapped out with my financial planner. Now, at least, I feel as if I have some direction."
~Kelly, a 45-year-old physician

4. Diversify

"I inherited a lot of stock in a corporation that was considered the Rock of Gibraltar of blue chips. My grandmother told me, 'Never sell this stock.' When the price dropped by half this year, I took an enormous hit and panicked. I hired a financial planner and she helped me select about a dozen mutual funds with different objectives. Now I understand why it's so important to spread your money around."
~Deena, a 25-year-old graduate student

5. Don't be afraid to make mistakes

"At first, if one of my stocks dropped, I'd think to myself, 'This is it; you're going to end up as a bag lady.' Now I take things in stride. I remind myself that investing is a process, and that my mistakes, which luckily haven't been costly, can be my best teachers."
~Charlene, a 38-year-old chemist

6. Be generous with yourself and others

"I used to feel so guilty about having inherited money that I pretended I didn't have it. But now that I've put so much work into learning how to manage my investments, I feel entitled to spend my money on things that give me pleasure — traveling, remodeling my house and supporting causes I care deeply about. But the biggest surprise to me is that I'm getting a kick out of investing."

~Sylvia, a 53-year-old architect

GLOSSARY

Allocation of assets: The division of money into stocks, bonds, real estate, cash and commodities.

American Stock Exchange (AMEX): The marketplace where mid-sized growth companies are traded.

Bear market: An extended period, usually one to three years, in which stock prices go down, usually due to negative economic factors.

Blue-chip companies: Large, quality companies noted for their records of financial stability and dividend payments.

Bond: An IOU or promissory note issued by a corporation, municipality, or the U.S. government and usually sold in multiples of $1,000.

Bull market: An extended period in which stock prices go up, usually as a result of positive economic factors.

Capital gain (loss): An increase (or decrease) in the dollar value of your investment.

Churn: Excessive trading in clients' accounts to generate commissions for stockbrokers.

Dividend: A payment of income, usually made quarterly, to stockholders of a corporation or mutual fund.

Dollar-cost averaging: A system of buying shares of mutual funds by investing fixed dollar amounts at regular intervals, regardless of the direction in which the market is moving.

Dow Jones Industrial Average (DJIA): A measure of stock market prices based on the performance of 30 leading manufacturing companies listed on the New York Stock Exchange.

Index: A statistical yardstick that measures a whole market by using a representative selection of stocks (the Dow Jones Industrial Average, S&P 500 Stock Index) or bonds (the Shearson Lehman Bond Index).

Limited partnership: A partnership in which some of the partners have only a limited liability for the partnership's obligations.

Load: The sales charge you pay a broker when you buy (or sometimes sell) certain mutual funds.

Mutual fund: A professionally managed, diversified portfolio of stocks and/or bonds, etc. in which investors' money is pooled to buy securities.

National Association of Securities Dealers Automated Quotation (NASDAQ): The electronic computer network brokers use to trade shares of companies listed on this exchange.

New York Stock Exchange (NYSE): The marketplace for large, established companies; also called "the Big Board."

Net asset value (NAV): The market value of each share of a mutual fund on any given day.

Net worth: The difference between the total value of what you own (your assets) and what you owe (your liabilities).

No-load mutual fund: A fund that does not include a sales commission when you buy or sell shares, although it does have built-in fees for marketing, management, and redemption that vary from fund to fund.

Portfolio: The securities you hold in an individual account or that are held by a mutual fund.

Portfolio manager: The money manager who buys and sells securities for individuals or for mutual funds.

Securities*:* A catchall term for various investment products like stocks, bonds, and mutual funds.

Securities analyst: Someone who researches information about stocks and bonds and evaluates whether or not they would be good investments.

Stock: Securities representing ownership in a company, sometimes paying dividends and giving you the right to vote on company issues.

Total return: The total change in value of an investment over a given period (usually one year) that results from both income (interest, dividends) and capital appreciation (change in fair market value from the purchase price).

Trade: To buy and sell stocks and bonds. A "trade" refers to the exchange that takes place when one person buys a security that someone else has sold.

Yield: The dividend or interest paid by a company, expressed as a percentage of the current price, or, if you own the security, the percentage of the price you originally paid.

ABOUT BARBARA STANNY

Barbara Stanny an accomplished inspirational speaker, best-selling author and wealth coach, is the leading authority on women and wealth. She is the author of *Sacred Success: A Course in Financial Miracles; Overcoming Underearning: A Five-Step Plan to a Richer Life; Secrets of Six Figure Women: Surprising Strategies To Up Your Earnings and Change Your Life and Prince Charming Isn't Coming: How Women Get Smart About Money.*

In addition to books, workshops and keynotes, Barbara has also developed *Secrets of Successful High Earners and Becoming Your Own Prince Charming*, two seminars-in-a-box for financial professionals, coaches and counselors, to present to help spread the message of personal and financial empowerment to women. She is the daughter of Richard Bloch, co-founder of H&R Block, and she lives in Port Townsend, Washington.

Barbara tours the country every year, appearing on television and speaking to various groups about empowering women financially. These are just a few highlights of her media appearances: Good Morning America, The View, Power Lunch on CNBC, Money Matters on CNN, MSNBC.com, Your World with Neil Cavuto and The O'Reilly Report, both on FOX News Channel.

To learn more visit www.BarbaraStanny.com

OTHER PRODUCTS

Available at www.BarbaraStanny.com

Books, Ebooks, Audiobooks, MP3, CD's

Sacred Success®: A Course in Financial Miracles (hardcover, Ebook, Audiobook on CD)
Secrets of Six-Figure Women®: Surprising Strategies to Up Your Earnings and Change your Life (paperback, Ebook)
Prince Charming Isn't Coming®: How Women Get Smart About Money (paperback, Ebook)
Finding a Financial Advisor You Can Trust: A Guide For Investors and Those Who Want To Be (paperback, MP3)
Overcoming Underearning®: A Five-Step Plan to a Richer Life (paperback, Ebook)
Guided Exercises for Overcoming Underearning: A Five-Step Plan to a Richer Life (CD, MP3)
Breaking Through: Getting Through the Suck Points in Your Life (paperback, Ebook)
Ideas to Contemplate from Breaking Through: Getting Through the Stuck Points in Your Life (CD, MP3)
Exercises and Action Steps from Breaking Through: Getting Though the Stuck Points in Your Life (CD, MP3)

More Products:

Sacred Success Retreat: *4 day/3 night intimate and eye-opening retreat with Barbara. Two per year one each on the East and West coasts.*
One Year to Wealth: Become a Savvy Investor: *In one simple step a month over a year Barbara will show you how to become a Wealth Builder.*

Overcoming Underearning Webinar: *A 5 week webinar that includes 4 recorded content sessions and 5 live sessions with Barbara.*

Coaching with Barbara: *Single session, 6 sessions, 12 sessions and group sessions available.*

Weekly Words of Wealth: *Sign up and get weekly emails so Barbara can help guide you to your path of prosperity.*

Monthly Money Mondays: *On the first Monday of every month, talk to Barbara for FREE!*

Barbara Stanny Mouse Pad: *Bright, bold and fun! It has three mantras printed on it: Scare yourself every day, Surround yourself with support, Make a difference in the world.*

To learn more or register visit www.BarbaraStanny.com

Made in the USA
San Bernardino, CA
04 April 2015